"This day proved the best we have had since at this place, only 3 showers of rain to day, cloudy nearly all day, in the evening the wind luled and the fore part of the night fair and clear   I saw flies and different kinds of insects in motion to day Snakes are yet to be seen and snales without cover is common and large."

William Clark
*Lewis & Clark Journal*
Fort Clatsop
December 30, 1805

# ORYGONE IV*

## or, if this is July and it's raining, this must be Oregon.

### By James Cloutier

IMAGE WEST PRESS · EUGENE, OREGON

* Orygone I and II are out of print which is to say they never were in.

My thanks to Bob Bury
for his quick and clever wit.

ISBN: 0-918966-03-5

Library of Congress Catalog No. 78-71301

Manufactured in the United States of America

Image West Press
Post Office Box 5511
Eugene, Oregon 97405

# Symbols of Oregon

### STATE SEAL
The state seal consists of a shield supported by 33 drops of rain and divided by an ordinary with the inscription, "The Onion." Above the ordinary, or ribbon, are the official seal and beautiful landscape of Oregon. Below the ribbon is Oregon's state animal, the ubiquitous slug. The Crest is the common seagull, frequently found near water and garbage dumps, perched on a common umbrella.

**STATE MOTTO** · The state motto, "The Onion" was adopted by the 1957 Legislature. Actually, it should have been "The Union" but the clerk was hard of hearing.

**STATE FISH** · After considerable debate the Grey back Mudsucker was declared State Fish by the 1961 Legislature. Coming in a close second was the Fathead Minnow.

**STATE TREE** · Swamp maple was designated Oregon's state tree in 1939.

**STATE SHRUB** · Poison oak was recently named Oregon State Shrub. It is generously available for tourists to take home with them in pots, bouquets or wreaths.

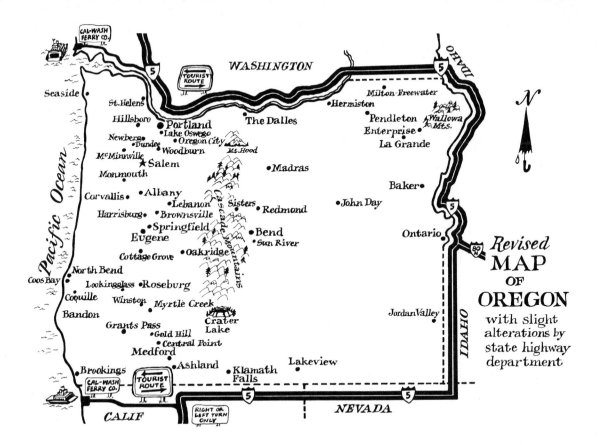

The moment you cross Oregon's border, you'll discover fine food and clean accomodations......

....welcome to
Vancouver, Washington

Visit Portland,
Oregon's fun city...

....why, people come here all the way from Gresham, Newberg and Oregon City.

When you visit
Oregon, be sure to
wear a coat with
a waterproof label...

...but not in the rain. The label's waterproof, not the coat.

It rained so long and hard in Oregon this year even the roses didn't bloom...

...don't miss Portland's famous Algae Festival Parade next June. (and learn the true meaning of the word "float".)

Oregon weather forecasters held their first annual picnic last summer...

*...unfortunately, it was rained out.*

Driving on Portland's 82<sup>nd</sup> avenue is like eating a watermelon...

....it would be much better if it wasn't so seedy.

Shopping in Lake Oswego can be expensive. At one supermarket lamb chops cost 6.95 a lb....

....that's if you rent them. (and they have to be returned the following day)

Spend an evening
on the town in wild,
exciting Woodburn...

....where they serve
martinis with a prune
instead of an olive.

The state highway
department is
concerned about
tourists getting lost
in Oregon...

...so, they've closed
all off-ramps on I-5.

See Salem, home of the state legislature, where you'll find a lot of political jokes...

...a few of them even
got elected.

If you're flying from Salem to Medford, take the economy flight...

...that's the one
that does a little crop
dusting along the way.

Last year thousands of Americans toured Russia behind the Iron Curtain...

...this year thousands
of tourists will travel
in Oregon behind the
Shower Curtain.

Stop over in Monmouth, a small community just west of Salem...

....it's also the wettest
dry town in Oregon.

Watch local government in action. Attend a city council meeting in Corvallis...

...meetings are held weekly in city hall over the Dairy Queen.

There's something about campus life at O.S.U. in Corvallis that really gets you....

...especially if you're standing downwind from the cow barns.

They're trying to harness a new form of energy in the Willamette Valley...

...it's called the "sneeze."

...when you visit there,
you won't believe the
condition of the air.

Lebanon is proud of its first gourmet restaurant. It opened last week....

...and already 2,600
Big Macs have sold.

Historic Brownsville
has a lot to offer...

...it's located on
Main street and
lists for $6,000.

If you get the urge to visit Oregon, spend a smoky summer in the Willamette Valley...

....if you have a burning desire to stay longer, buy a grass seed farm near Harrisburg.

Eugene is a friendly university town where people enjoy jogging up hills....

....and running
down tourists.

If you don't like
the way people drive
in Eugene.....

....then quit jogging
on the sidewalk.

If the rain in Oregon disturbs you, you can either see a psychiatrist or ride a bicycle....

*......in other words,*
*shrink or schwinn.*

Last summer 15,126 out-of-state visitors attended Springfield's Broiler Festival...

..... unfortunately,
15,000 were chickens
from Arkansas.

Oakridge is a quiet small town in the mountains....

...in fact, it's so small that when someone turns on tv, the street light dims.

In Oregon the flood waters always recede during the day only to return in the evening...

...that's when everyone wrings out their socks.

Go backpacking in Oregon's high Cascades. It's an unforgettable experience...

...you'll never forget
the mosquito bites over
the poison oak on top of
your sunburn.

Come to Cottage Grove for Bohemia Mining Days. You can no longer take gold out of the mine....

...but, hey...buy a used car in town and you can still get the shaft.

Jogging is becoming popular in Roseburg. Don't miss their annual Logger/Jogger Marathon...

...also known as the
Red Neck Run-off.

People in Oregon
don't really jog....

...they just wade,
wallow or slosh.

Downtown Lookingglass experienced a blackout last summer...

...someone unplugged
the extension cord
to the streetlight.

...they throw a big party every weekend.

Residents of Myrtle Creek spent last Christmas in Las Vegas...

....they had to. The town floated south for the winter.

Grants Pass is a
small pleasant town.
The Rogue River
passes right through it...

...and so do most
tourists.

When you visit the Oregon Caves, you'll find them dark, damp and cold...

...and your guide will
gladly let you know
when you're back outside.
(even if you have to call
 collect from Portland.)

If you're driving south on I-5, turn off at Gold Hill or Central Point....

...they've been turning
off tourists for years.

Each summer Medford attracts millions of visitors....

...a couple of dozen tourists and about ten million fruit flies.

While in Southern Oregon, attend the Shakespearean Festival. For a list of other exciting things to do in Ashland, turn the page...

There's a place just out of Klamath Falls where you can stop for food and gas...

...food when you arrive
and gas about two hours
down the road.

You'll enjoy the flight from Lakeview to Milton-Freewater...

...of course, you may
have to stop over in
John Day to give your
arms a rest.

There's considerable highway construction going on around Sunriver......

...they're building an
off and on ramp to
the L.A. freeway.

Last year in Oregon hundreds of thousands of people observed Ground Hog Day...

.....that's when all the
ex-Californians went
out to find their shadow.

Skiers and tourist resorts in Bend have something in common...

...they've been going downhill for years.

Don't miss
the Sisters Rodeo...

...that's where cowboys
ride on wild bulls and
fall off tame bar stools.

This winter spend a weekend at the Redmond Hotel....

...where it gets so cold they have to put anti-freeze in the waterbeds.

Madras is so dry in
the summer...

...even the cat fish have
ticks. (and wear goggles
to keep sand out of their
eyes.)

Each summer residents
of Pendleton anxiously
look forward to the
Round Up Parade...

...that's the only time
all year the streets get
cleaned.

Hermiston doesn't have any traffic problems...

...the speed limit there
is zero and they have
a law against backing up.

A cowboy in Enterprise was recently hit on the head by a drop of rain and knocked out...

...it took six buckets
of dust to revive him.

Folks in Eastern Oregon can tell when a duststorm is coming...

...they just listen
for the sneezing of
rattlesnakes.

In the Wallowa Mountains there are two kinds of mosquitoes: the small kind that come through a hole in your screen door...

*...and the big kind that open your screen door.*

If the constant rain
in Western Oregon
depresses you, go to
LaGrande to forget...

...then go to Baker
to forget LaGrande.

The Eastern Oregon
town of Ontario is in
a different time zone...

...so, when you go there, don't forget to set your watch back 75 years.

*Jordan Valley finally received electricity last week...*

...and they won't
get anymore until the
next big thunderstorm.

There's a small town in Eastern Oregon where you'll find little difference between the sheriff and chief of police....

...about one year of
high school.

Looking for fun and
excitement? Come to
The Dalles....

....people here have
been looking for fun
and excitement since
1854. (and they need all
the help they can get)

During yesterday's thunderstorm, all the windows were left open in Portland's big downtown hotel...

...and now it's the largest waterbed warehouse in Oregon.

Amtrak is finally speeding up its service between Portland and Eugene....

*...they're moving the stations closer together.*

St. Helens is certainly a progressive growing town....

*...just last week they got their first Edsel dealership.*

Eating out in
Hillsboro is a real
experience....

..the town's only deli specializes in pastrami on raisin bread with mayonnaise.

Tour the wineries in Dundee. You'll find them surprisingly clean...

...even the restrooms
have signs that read,
"Employees must wash
feet before leaving."

McMinnville nearly had to cancel its Turkey-Rama last summer. They couldn't find enough turkeys....

....but, luckily, two county commissioners returned early from their vacations.

Hot air ballooning is becoming popular in Oregon, especially around Salem....

...but only when the legislature is in session.

Buying a house in Oregon is easy, especially in the winter.....

...that's when any-
body can float a
loan.

Want to get away from seedy tourist resorts and tacky souvenir stands? Come to Seaside....

...anywhere you go from here will be away from seedy tourist resorts and tacky souvenir stands.

If you get lost while visiting Oregon, just ask someone for directions....

*....Oregonians enjoy telling tourists where to go.*

North Bend has a classy motel that offers a room and bath for $8.50....

...unfortunately, they're in different buildings.

In Coos Bay there are several motels to select from...

....the most expensive
one features a bridal
suite with bunk beds.

In Oregon we depend
on the rain to keep our
logs moving downstream...

...which may explain
why so many end up
in Japan.

There's a foreign economical import that's been saving gas in Oregon for years...

...it's called the
Australian crawl.

In Coquille it only floods once a year...

...the other three
months it's not bad
at all.

Many old timers reside in Bandon, the Cranberry Capital of the world....

...in fact, people have
been bogged down there
for years.

Keeping Oregon clean and green is easy....

...the rain washes the streets and the mildew takes care of the rest.

...even the town drunk's wife won't let him in until he's wiped his hands and knees.

When *you* visit Oregon, don't forget Noah's last words as he sailed off in the ark....

...."Why does it always
rain on my vacation?"